Chronicle of Books

GW01270021

Sallie Purkis

This is a reference book. You can use it to find out how books were made, who read them and what the writing and pictures looked like.

Contents

How the Chronicles are organised

The Chronicles are organised into parts. This is because history is easier to understand if we divide it into parts called **periods**. These periods are sections of time in history.

This book has been organised into 13 periods. Each period has a starting date and an ending date. Of course, we cannot always say exactly when one period ends and another starts, so the dates are just a guide.

The choice of periods

Each of the Chronicles in the Longman Book Project cover the same 13 periods of history. To help you remember the periods, there is a special memorable event for each one shown in the top right hand corner.

Subheadings

On each page there are a number of headings and subheadings. The subheadings are the same for each period. This helps you to compare facts about books from one period with facts about books from another period.

The timeline

On the bottom of each page there is a timeline. The timeline stretches from Roman times to the present day. There was plenty of history **before** Roman times but it is not covered in this book.

AD | 1500

How to use the book for research

You can use the Chronicle to compare information from one period with another. For instance, you might want to compare famous books written in one period with those written in another. If this is all you need to know, you can just read the information under these subheadings and ignore the rest of the writing.

How to use the Chronicles to cross-reference

You might want to research using more than one of the Chronicles in the Longman Book Project. You can easily do this, because each Chronicle covers the same periods in history. You can therefore compare the information in one Chronicle with that in another.

How the books were made

Books in Roman times were written by hand. They were written on paper made from a plant called 'papyrus'. The paper was rolled into a scroll. There were no pages, just columns of writing on the scroll. Most scrolls were about 10 metres long.

The Romans thought that papyrus was too thin, so by about AD 300 scrolls were made from parchment. Parchment was made from animal skins, and it was much thicker than papyrus.

What the writing looked like

The Romans wrote in Latin, which was the language they spoke. They were the first people to write in letters which had curves as well as straight lines. This is called 'cursive writing'.

A Roman pen was called a stylus and was made from pieces of metal, bones or reeds. The Romans used ink made from soot and gum.

What the pictures were like

Nobody knows for certain what the pictures were like in Ancient Roman books, as no pictures have lasted until today.

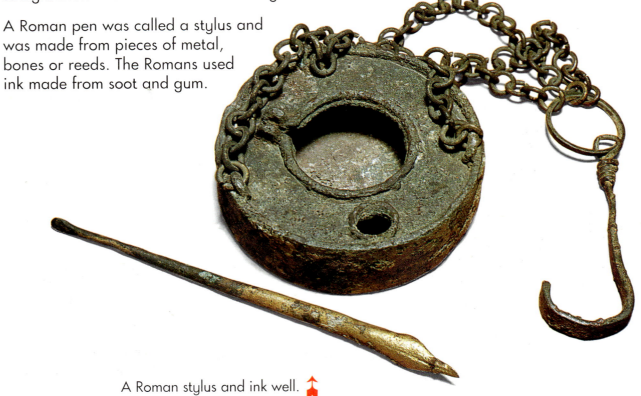

A Roman stylus and ink well.

AD|01   AD|500   A

What sort of books were written

The Romans wrote many different kinds of books. We know they wrote law books, account books, poetry books and history books, because some of them have been found.

Parts of the New Testament of the Bible were written in Roman times.

Who read the books

Not many people could read in Roman times, and books cost a lot of money. Children who went to school read books by Roman and Greek writers.

Famous books

One famous book was written by Julius Caesar. It was about the first invasions of Britain in 55 and 54 BC.

Tacitus wrote a history book about Britain, and Virgil wrote poems about wars and about the Italian countryside.

 Boys learnt to read from scrolls at Roman schools.

How the books were made

Books in Anglo-Saxon times were written on sheets of parchment, which were made from the dried skins of goats, sheep or calves.

Four sheets of parchment were folded to make sixteen pages. These were called quires. The quires were then made into books, with covers made from wood or leather.

What the writing looked like

Nuns and monks wrote with quill pens made from feathers. They wrote in a round and flowing style.

What the pictures were like

Some books had paintings of scenes from the Bible, and sometimes there were pictures of the monks and nuns themselves.

The first letter on some pages was decorated with a pattern. This was called an illuminated letter.

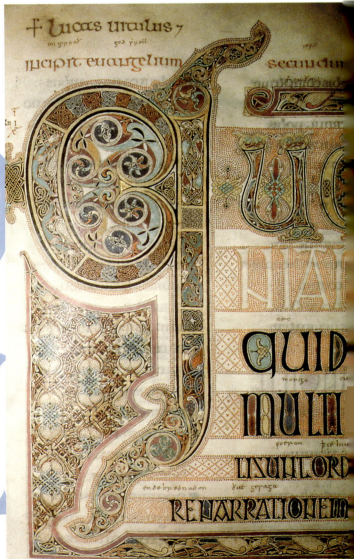

An illuminated letter in an Anglo-Saxon book. ➤➤

What sort of books were written

In Anglo-Saxon times many people in Britain were Christians. The Bible was the most common book. Only the monks and nuns knew how to write and they used to copy out the Bible. Some of them also wrote history books and books about what was happening in the world.

Who read the books

The Bible was usually read aloud to teach people about Christianity. Not many people could read, but some boys and girls went to schools run by monks and nuns.

Famous books

A monk called Bede wrote books. His most famous book is called *A History of the English Church and People.*

Other monks wrote *The Anglo-Saxon Chronicle,* which was about things that happened each year.

Beowulf was a poem which told an exciting story.

 An Anglo-Saxon monk writing in a library.

How the books were made

No books written by the Vikings have been found. In those days people told each other stories instead of reading them or writing them down. Some Viking writing has been found carved on stones or scratched on metal.

What the writing looked like

Viking letters were all made with straight lines because they were carved, and not written with a pen and ink. The letters are called 'runes'.

What the pictures were like

The Vikings often carved patterns that looked like pieces of ribbon on the stones. In the patterns were pictures of strange animals and serpents. Some stones had pictures of Viking heroes, heroines, gods and goddesses.

Viking runes and patterns carved onto stone.

Why the runes were written

Rune stones were put up to honour friends and relations who had died. They may have told people about things the dead person believed in and about the gods they worshipped.

Who read the runes

No one knows who read the messages on the stones.

Famous Viking stories

Many stories were told about Viking gods and goddesses like Woden, who was also called Odin, Thor and Freya. Some of our days of the week – Wednesday, Thursday and Friday – are named after these gods and goddesses.

This rune stone shows the god Odin attacked by a fierce dog.

How the books were made

The Normans wrote their books on sheets of parchment, as the Anglo-Saxons had done. The pages were sewn together, and a leather cover was put round them. This was called a binding.

What the writing looked like

The Normans wrote either in Latin or in French. They used quill pens made from feathers, and they could write with curves as well as with straight lines.

What the pictures were like

Some of the books had no pictures, but certain words and headings were underlined in red ink. In other books some capital letters were decorated with coloured patterns and small pictures. These were called illuminated letters.

An illuminated letter from a twelfth-century Bible in Winchester Cathedral Library. ➤➤

TENENS

AD 01   AD 500   A

What sort of books were written

In 1085 King William sent some clerks round the country with a list of questions. They had to write down who owned the land, if it was forest, farming or marsh land, the number of buildings and animals in each village, and what everything was worth. People called this the *Domesday Book*.

Books of prayers and the Bible were also copied out by clerks working in the 'scriptorium', or writing room, in monasteries and cathedrals.

Who read the books

The information collected by King William's clerks was kept in books in his Treasury. William used the books to help him collect taxes.

Copies of the Bible and prayer books were either bought by rich people living in castles, or kept in churches.

Famous books

The most famous Norman book is really two books. Inside them is all the information collected for King William. The two books are called the *Domesday Book*.

 This is what the *Domesday Book* looks like today.

How the books were made

All books in Britain were written by hand until 1476. Most of them were still written on parchment or vellum, but during the fourteenth century people learnt how to make paper from old rags.

What the writing looked like

The best scribes drew careful lines and wrote with thin and thick strokes of the pen.

What the pictures were like

Artists drew people at work and at home. Some medical books had pictures of the human body, and others showed which plants and herbs were good for making medicines. Pictures of animals were also very popular.

 This book from the Middle Ages shows a woman milking a cow.

What sort of books were written

Rich men and women paid scribes and clerks to write books for them to have at home. They usually chose books of prayers, songs, or poems.

Who read the books

Only men or women who had been to a monastery or cathedral school or to one of the new universities could read. They were often called 'scholars'. People who could not read learnt the prayers, songs and poems by heart.

 Sir Geoffrey Luttrell and his family having a meal, from the prayer book called the *Luttrell Psalter*.

Famous books

The Canterbury Tales is a long poem about pilgrims going from London to Canterbury.

Stories of popular heroes like Robin Hood were written down for the first time.

Prayer books, with pictures of the countryside at each season of the year, were called 'Books of Hours'.

Books of animal pictures were called 'Bestiaries' or 'Beast' books.

The *Luttrell Psalter* was a prayer book written for the Luttrell family. In it are pictures of life in Lincolnshire, where the family lived.

How the books were made

In 1476 a man called William Caxton used a printing press for the first time in Britain. Metal letters, called type, were put together to make words. Ink was put on the type-face, which was then pressed down hard onto paper. This was an important invention, because many copies of a book could be printed from the same type, whereas previously books could only be handwritten one at a time.

What the writing looked like

The first printers used letters in the Gothic style – the same sort of letters that the manuscript writers had used. The metal letters were called moveable type, because they could be moved about and used over and over again to make lots of different words.

*for whyche he had ...
for his largenes & f...
That wonder was ...
Amonge all thyse g...
Ther was a mon...
I trowe that .rrr. wy...
That euer in one w...*

What the pictures were like

Pictures were cut on blocks of wood. They were called woodcuts. They had to be carved back to front, like an image in a mirror. When they were printed, the right image came out on the paper. The first printers only knew how to use one colour of ink on each block.

One of the first printing presses. It was operated by hand.

What sort of books were written

Many different kinds of books were printed. The Bible, poems, plays, stories, and recipes for making medicines from herbs were all popular. You did not have to be very rich to buy a book. Books were sold on market stalls and by pedlars in the street.

Who read the books

More people than ever before learnt to read, although this was still only a small part of the population. At school many children read books in Greek and Latin, as well as in English.

Famous books

The Canterbury Tales by Geoffrey Chaucer, written between 1387 and 1400, was one of the first books printed by William Caxton.

The Bible was translated into English for the first time, and many copies were printed.

A page from *The Canterbury Tales* by Geoffrey Chaucer, printed by William Caxton. You can see the Gothic letters and the picture printed from a woodcut.

How the books were made

Books in Stuart times were printed on paper. The paper was made by hand from wet linen rags. Small cheap books, called 'chapbooks', did not have a cover but expensive books were sent to bookbinders to have leather covers put on.

What the writing looked like

Printers found that they could buy many different styles of type. They chose letters which looked more like the letters we use today. The big difference was that sometimes the letter '*s*' looked like our letter '*f*'.

What the pictures were like

Pictures were still printed from woodcuts in one colour (usually black), but printers could also buy type with patterns or borders to decorate the pages.

Progrefs

In the first libraries, the books were chained to the bookshelves.

What sort of books were written

The first bookshops were called stationers' shops, where you bought things printed on paper. People liked to buy books about science, books of poetry, and plays. During the Civil War, both the Royalists and the Parliamentarians wrote books to tell people their opinions and points of view.

Who read the books

A lot more people could read. The first libraries were built in colleges and schools in Stuart times.

Famous books

William Shakespeare is famous for writing a lot of plays. They were first printed in Stuart times.

The Pilgrim's Progress was written by John Bunyan. It is the story of an imaginary journey through life. The hero, Christian, has to decide which way to go.

Two men, John Evelyn and Samuel Pepys, wrote diaries at this time, but the diaries were not printed for people to read until two hundred years later.

 A picture of Christian, the hero of the book *The Pilgrims's Progress*.

THE
Pilgrim's Progress
FROM
THIS WORLD,
TO
That which is to come

Delivered under the Similitude of a

DREAM

Wherein is Discovered,
The Manner of his setting out,
His Dangerous JOURNEY,
AND
Safe Arrival at the Desired Countrey.

By JOHN BUNYAN.

The Third Edition, with Additions.

I have used Similitudes, *Hosea*, 12. 10.

Licensed and Entred according to Order.

LONDON,
Printed for *Nath. Ponder*, at the *Peacock* in the *Poultrey* near *Cornhil*, 1679.

How the books were made

Books were made in the same way as in earlier times. However in the eighteenth century the covers of some leather-bound books were lined with paper decorated with a marble pattern. In 1798 a machine was invented in France to make paper from wood pulp instead of from linen rags. This made paper much cheaper.

What the writing looked like

Two Englishmen called Mr Caslon and Mr Baskerville, who lived in Worcestershire, designed some new type-faces, which were plain and easy to read. Printers still use the letters they designed today.

What the pictures were like

Most pictures in books were still made from woodcuts. Sometimes the black and white prints were coloured by hand, particularly in children's books. The books with coloured pictures cost more.

Bath,

One of the first printed children's books. It was called *Mother Goose's Melody*.

What sort of books were written

Very rich people began to collect books to create and build libraries in their homes. They collected old books written by the Greeks and the Romans, as well as books written in the Seventeenth Century. These included some of the first travel books, books about science, and the first long novels.

Who read the books

People used to read books for information and for entertainment. The first children's books were printed, but not many children could read, so the books were read to them by their mothers and fathers.

Famous Books

The first *English Dictionary* was written by Dr Samuel Johnson.

Daniel Defoe wrote a desert island story called *Robinson Crusoe* and Jonathan Swift wrote about imaginary places in a book called *Gulliver's Travels*.

Sleeping Beauty, Puss-in-Boots, Cinderella, Tom Thumb and *Jack the Giant-Killer* were some of the first fairy stories to appear in children's books.

 Robinson Crusoe on his desert island.

↑ The title page of a book of *Grimm's Fairy stories*.

How the books were made

Many new machines were invented at this time. One was a printing press which worked by steam power. It could print books four times faster than an old hand-press. It also printed double pages, instead of one page at a time. Printers were now so busy that they had no time to find authors, artists and bookbinders. This job was taken over by new people in the book trade, called publishers.

What the writing looked like

Plain type-faces that were easy to read were chosen for most books.

THE "ORIGINAL POEMS" AND OTHERS

What the pictures were like

Drawings were scratched with thin lines on to copper plates. When acid was spread over the drawings, some of the copper dissolved. A block for printing was left. Pictures made from these blocks were called etchings.

What sort of books were written

Jane Austen and Sir Walter Scott were famous authors from this time. Many adults enjoyed reading their novels. The first fairy stories written for children were translated from German and published in Britain. The first story about a family, called *The Swiss Family Robinson,* was published in 1814.

Who read the books

There were still only a few schools, but some children learnt to read at home. Anyone who wanted to borrow books instead of buying them paid a sum of money each year to join a circulating library.

Famous books

Sir Walter Scott wrote stories about Scottish history.

Sense and Sensibility and *Pride and Prejudice* were two of the novels written by Jane Austen, and people still enjoy reading them today.

Snow White and *Hansel and Gretel* were two stories in a new book of fairy stories collected by the Grimm brothers in Germany. The stories were translated into English in 1823.

A title page from a book of poems by Ann and Jane Taylor. The publisher's name is at the bottom of the page.

How the books were made

A rotary printing press was invented, and this printed books even faster than before. It was a cylinder with type moulded on to the side, and it was covered with ink and rolled over the paper. Other cylinders, with coloured ink on them, printed the pictures. Another machine stuck the pages into a case, or cover, which was made of a special cloth.

What the writing looked like

There were no big changes in the way type-faces looked.

What the pictures were like

The first books with printed coloured pictures were published in 1835. Two or three colours could be printed, but this process took a long time, as only one colour could be printed at a time.

"Well, then," the (went on, "you see a (growls when it's ang and wags its tail when pleased. Now *I* growl wl I'm pleased, and wag tail when I'm angry. The fore I'm mad."

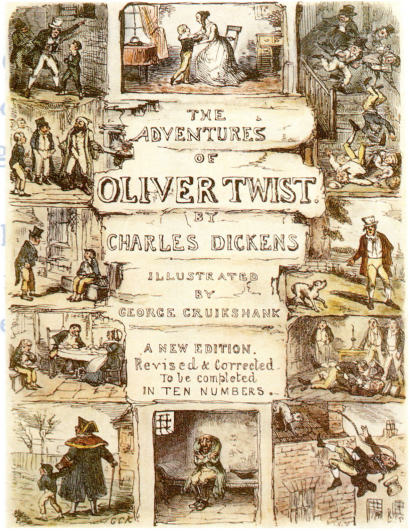

Oliver Twist, by Charles Dickens, ➤➤ was about an orphan boy who started life in the workhouse.

What sort of books were written

A lot of books were written for the new schools which were being built in all parts of the country. Other books were written in instalments: readers bought a new part of the book every week, until they had collected the whole book.

Who read the books

There were no TVs or radios at this time, so reading books was very popular. The first public libraries were opened by town councils. Books were bought from the council taxes which were called the 'rates', and everyone living in the town could borrow the books.

Famous books

Charles Dickens was the most popular writer of this time – even Queen Victoria read his books. *A Christmas Carol, Oliver Twist* and *David Copperfield* are three of the books written by Dickens.

Fairy tales collected by Hans Andersen included *The Tinder Box, The Ugly Duckling* and *The Twelve Dancing Princesses*.

Robert Browning wrote the long story-poem called *The Pied Piper*.

Edward Lear's *Book of Nonsense Rhymes* was first on sale in 1842.

Tom Brown's Schooldays was a book about life at Rugby, a boy's boarding school.

Lewis Carroll wrote two stories called *Alice's Adventures in Wonderland* and *Through the Looking Glass*.

Black Beauty, the story about the life of a horse, became a bestseller about 1873.

The Cheshire cat who smiled is one character that Alice met during her adventures in Wonderland.

How the books were made

The most important invention at this time was the linotype machine. It had a keyboard rather like a typewriter or a computer today. It made a whole line of words into one piece of type. When the printing was finished, the metal type was melted down to make new lines of type.

What the writing looked like

The type-faces in books looked almost the same as they do today. There was one important exception – an artist called William Morris used Gothic type on a hand-press, just as the first English printer, William Caxton, had done five hundred years previously.

What the pictures were like

Pictures to go in books were first drawn with fine pencil lines by artists, and sometimes they were painted with water-colours. Printers took photographs of the drawings and paintings, and turned them into printing blocks.

❧ Two hund
printed with
«Arches» lir
at five shill
nan vellu

A APPLE PIE

◀◀ Kate Greenaway was famous for her books of poetry for children which were illustrated with her own paintings.

What sort of books were written

After 1870 every child had to go to school. Mathematics, geography, history and science books were needed, as well as books which helped children to learn how to read.

People wanted books on many different subjects. Books with titles like *Enquire Within About Everything, The Home Doctor* and *Mrs Beeton's Book of Cookery and Household Management* were used at home.

Who read the books

For the first time in history, almost everyone could read. People could now choose books which they liked or which provided them with information.

 Sherlock Holmes and his friend Dr Watson solved crimes in books written by Arthur Conan Doyle.

Famous books

Arthur Conan Doyle wrote some crime stories with a detective called Sherlock Holmes as the hero.

Treasure Island, by Robert Louis Stevenson, was an adventure story about pirates. Stevenson also wrote a famous poetry book for children, called *A Child's Garden of Verses.*

The Jungle Book, by Rudyard Kipling, was a collection of animal stories.

The Tale of Peter Rabbit was a story book for young children. It was written by Beatrix Potter, and illustrated with paintings done by her too.

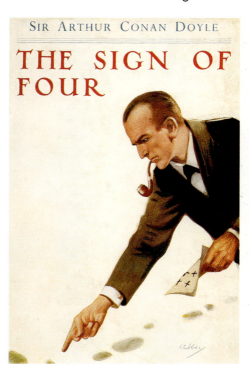

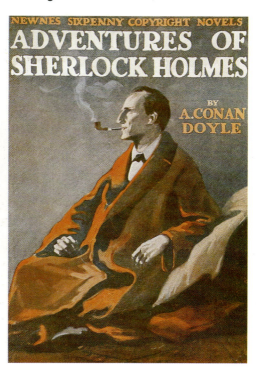

How the books were made

By this time all books were made in factories. Machines did the printing and put on the covers. Thousands of copies of every book were stored in big warehouses before being packed up and sent to bookshops all over the world.

What the writing looked like

There were machines to print books in different styles, with different colours, and in different sizes of print, and even in different languages.

What the pictures were like

Paintings and drawings looked almost as good on the printed page as they did in the artists' sketch-book. The first black and white photographs also appeared in books.

In the book *The Wind in the Willows,* Rat and Mole have a picnic.

AD 01   AD 500   A

What sort of books were written

Books were as important then as TV is today. Readers wanted to carry books about with them, so some publishers printed small-sized books called 'pocket' books. A famous series which was started at this time was called 'Everyman's Library', and it included many famous books from the past like *The Canterbury Tales* and *The Pilgrim's Progress*.

Who read the books

Most people knew how to read by this time, and so there was a very big market for books. They were on sale in shops in every high street and at bookstalls at every railway station. While out shopping many people called in at Boots (the chemist), which had its own library in over 400 branches of the shop all over the country.

Famous books

The Railway Children, by E. Nesbit, which has now been made into a film, was a popular children's book in 1906.

Peter Pan, by James Barrie, was an adventure story written for a family of children whom he knew well.

The Wind in the Willows, which has now been made into a cartoon film, was written in 1908.

The *Dr Doolittle* books came out in 1920.

The first stories about the teddy bear Winnie the Pooh were published in 1926.

How the books are made

There have been many changes in the way books are made since 1930. The first paperbacks were published by Penguin Books in 1935. They were made very cheaply, and sold for only 6d (about 3p in today's money). Puffin Books for children were introduced by the same firm five years later.

Today books are often printed on computers, and people can even do their own desk-top publishing at home or in a small office.

What the writing looks like

Nowadays there are thousands of different type-faces and many different ways of printing to choose from.

What the pictures are like

The first coloured photographs appeared in books in about 1960, but artists are still employed to draw pictures for many books.

Writing
Writing
Writing
WRITING
WRITING
Writing
Writing
WRITING
Writing
WRITING

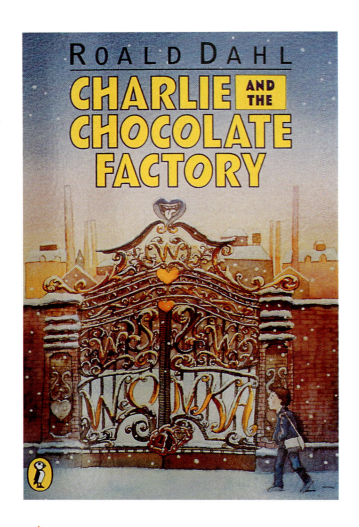

 Roald Dahl was a best-selling writer of children's books.

What sort of books are written

Many new novels are written every year for adults and for children. Some of them are made into films.

Books that go with TV programmes sell very well. Reference and information books are also popular.

Several prizes are given to authors and illustrators every year for good books.

Who reads the books

Watching TV and films, and listening to music are now more popular pastimes than reading books. We can buy cassettes and listen to books being read. Some famous books have been made into films, cartoons for TV and videos. However good books are still popular with people of all age groups.

Famous books

Agatha Christie's crime stories are very popular. Readers enjoy following the detectives Hercule Poirot and Miss Marple whom she writes about.

Many famous authors have written and are writing books for children today. Roald Dahl is very well-known, and most children have read *Charlie and the Chocolate Factory* and *James and the Giant Peach*. Other popular children's writers include Michael Rosen, John Agard, Anne Fine and Nicholas Fisk.

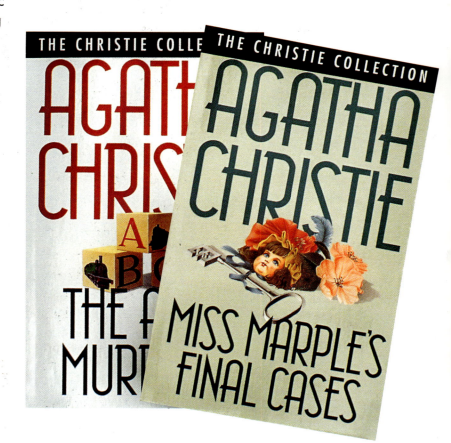

The Miss Marple stories have now been made into films and shown on television.

GLOSSARY

Chapbook — A chapbook is a small book which was sold by pedlars in Tudor and Stuart times.

Clerk — A clerk was a priest or monk in the Middle Ages who knew how to write.

Cursive — Cursive letters had curved edges.

Etching — An etching was a picture printed from a scratched metal plate.

Gothic — Gothic letters were designed with thick lines and angular corners.

Illuminated — Illuminated means decorated. This word is usually used to describe the first letter on a manuscript page.

Instalment — An instalment is part of a long serial story.

Linotype — Linotype is a whole line of metal type used for printing.

Manuscript — A manuscript is a handwritten book or document.

Paperback — A paperback is a book with a soft cover made from card or paper.

Papyrus — Papyrus is a tall plant with wide leaves which were used to make paper in ancient times.

Parchment — Parchment is goat or sheep skin specially prepared to write on.

Press — A press is a machine used for printing letters, words and pictures from a block onto paper.

Publisher — A publisher is a person or company which produces books and arranges to sell them.

Quill — A quill is a pen made from a goose feather. The point was cut with a penknife.

Quire — A quire was a set of sheets fitted together to make a book.

Runes — Runes were Saxon and Viking letters.

Scroll — A scroll is a roll of parchment.

Stylus — A stylus is a pen made from a piece of wood or metal with a point.

Type — Type is metal letters mounted on a block so that they can be printed in a press.

Vellum — Vellum is very fine quality pig, goat or calf skin specially prepared for writing or making book covers.

Woodcut — A woodcut is a picture printed from a carved wooden block.

FURTHER INFORMATION

Books

To find out more about the technology of making books, use a good encyclopaedia and look up words like 'printing' and 'bookbinding'.

You can find out more about the authors of famous books in an encyclopaedia too or in the *Dictionary of National Biography*.

The famous books have been reprinted many times. Look for a copy in your local library.

Visits

Old books do not survive very well. Museums keep them in a glass case covered with a cloth as the colours fade if the light gets to them. Visitors lift back the cloth to look at the old book and then cover it up again.

If you visit a country house where a rich family lived in the past you will be shown the library. Look at the old books bound with leather, the shelves which were built for the books and the other special furniture.

INDEX

a b c d e f g h i j k l m n o p q r s t u v w x y z
A B C D E F G H I J K L M N O P Q R S T U V W X Y Z